Bad Manners
Nick Baker

SPHERE

SPHERE BOOKS LIMITED
London & Sydney

Also by Nick Baker
in Sphere Books
BAD LOSERS
(with Brian Busselle)

First published by Sphere Books Ltd, 1985
30-32 Gray's Inn Road, London WC1X 8JL
Copyright © 1985 by Nick Baker and Brian
Busselle

To Jill and Angie

TRADE
MARK

SPHERE

Reproduced, printed and bound in Great Britain
by Hazell Watson & Viney Limited, Aylesbury,
Bucks

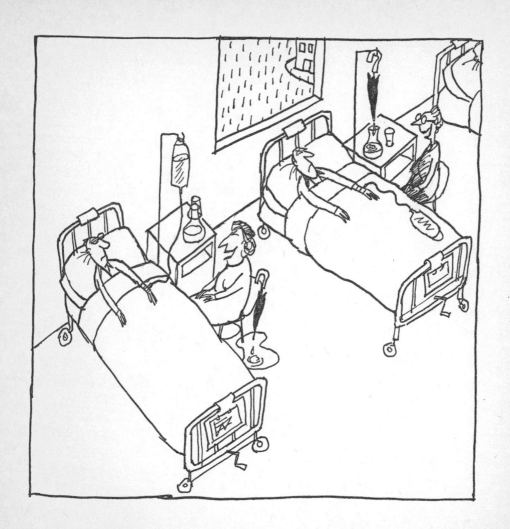

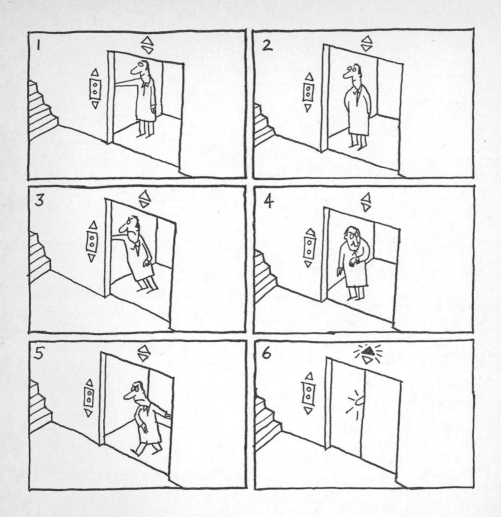